Copyright © Marcy Stone 201

All rights reserved. No part of this book may be reproduced in any form without permission in writing from the author. Reviewers may quote brief passages in reviews.

DISCLAIMER

No part of this publication may be reproduced or transmitted in any form or by any means, mechanical or electronic, including photocopying or recording, or by any information storage and retrieval system, or transmitted by email without permission in writing from the author.

Neither the author nor the publisher assumes any responsibility for errors, omissions, or contrary interpretations of the subject matter herein. Any perceived slight of any individual or organization is purely unintentional.

Brand and product names are trademarks or registered trademarks of their respective owners.

ISBN: 9781791654207

Cover Layout by: Walter Stanley of Stanley Graphic Arts

Edits & Proofing: Judy Lantz & Aubrey Nicole Riegel

The Best of Both Worlds Cookbook

DEDICATION

Honoring our "foodies" that have passed,
benefiting the foodies of the future

We have taken traditional recipes, many in tribute from friends that have also lost a loved one, and converted them into healthier versions of themselves. Demonstrating that you are able to eat healthy and still have all the great flavors your palate and memories long for. Life is sweet, and with no guarantees so eat cake... and THEN eventually you may get to the entrée. It's about slowing down and having a little fun with the people you love.

The Best of Both Worlds Cookbook

The Best of Both Worlds Cookbook

Heavenly Recipes with a Healthy Twist

By Ken Bell & Marcy Stone

The Best of Both Worlds Cookbook

Table of Contents

Introduction	1
Sweet Fancy Treats	15
Libations	51
Munchies	63
Satisfying Sides, Soups, Stuffin's & Sauces	77
Delectable Dishes	93
Tricks & "Truisms"	115
Thank you	119
About the Authors	121

The Best of Both Worlds Cookbook

The Best of Both Worlds Cookbook

Introduction

The order of this cookbook...

...is very unconventional. In fact, according to every cookbook that I have seen, it is completely backwards! Who starts a meal with dessert? Most children would be extremely happy about starting with dessert and that is why we have done so! We are honoring the sweetness in life and feeding our inner child, the part of us that gets swept aside to be a mature, responsible adult!

This very unique cookbook is also about honoring our lost loved ones, about doing things different and breaking from the norm. Life is sweet, so eat cake... and THEN maybe get to the entrée. It's about having a little fun in an otherwise very serious and rule-ridden society. I dare you to serve your meal differently! Go against the grain, create new traditions, be adventurous. Do be sure make the portions a more reasonable size to ensure the remainder of the meal stands a chance.

Having lived with two foodies in my life, our daughter, Sydney, sadly now in heaven and my husband, Ken, there is a concept that I am very familiar with, "1st lunch & 2nd lunch". Of course then that also means that yep, you guessed it! "1st dinner & 2nd dinner!" For true diehard foodies, starting your meal with dessert is not a concern and the ability to pace your grazing, done wisely, can be very good for you overall. Small meals, like 1st and 2nd lunch are good for your metabolism as well as being able to benefit from these yummy morsels. It's when you "supersize" your portions that you get in trouble!

We have become a society of "supersizing", unlimited refills and cooking from a box. Please understand that I too made similar mistakes early in my daughters' lives so I understand completely. But I learned that none of these are healthy options nor are they good ways to teach our children to care for themselves. It troubles me when I hear people say things like, "I am too busy" or "organic is too expensive". I bet you anything that everyone who has a recipe dedicated in this book would tell you otherwise. Food used to be about spending time together as a family, cooking with love and slowing down and stay connected in an otherwise hectic day. For everyone who has dedicated a recipe in the following pages, "food triggers happy memories". They took the time to be together and now today, are forever grateful for those moments. They treasure them and relive them each time they prepare their favorite foods.

Being Mindful

We eat on the run, inhale our food and do not take the time to be thankful for our food, especially, if at one time, our food had a pulse. Be mindful to stop and give thanks to the farmers that took the time to diligently raise their crops and herds as well as the people that prepare the meals that you eat. This could be at your favorite restaurant or at your mother's or with your family. For those that enjoy cooking, there is nothing better than knowing that the food you patiently prepared with focused attention and unconditional love has been thoroughly savored.

This cookbook is not to convert you to veganism. It is simply to show how easy it is to eat healthier and a conversion in a recipe doesn't have to be intimidating. It is truly about perspective and thinking outside of the box from which you are familiar. You can eat organic and still eat meat or poultry. The trick is to be educated and mindful of how and where the product is being supplied. Many cattle herders today not only feed their cattle healthier but are more humane in their processing. Becoming more aware is the first step to living healthier and improving your quality of life from a nutritional standpoint.

Our Legacy

Being a momma bear, it is super important to me that our children become better and healthier in their lives. And they do so by watching us, their parents. We decided to honor our children, your children, by staging this book backwards. While our children look to us for examples of how to be the best person they can be. We can learn from them how to have more fun along the way. That seems like a pretty fair trade and crazy important in the quality and longevity of life, along with your food choices of course!

Throughout this cookbook we have taken recipes that people have lovingly provided to honor someone dear to them, and we have converted them into healthier versions of themselves. This is not saying that the original recipe is unhealthy. We are simply taking each recipe to a different level of healthy to show another alternative. Eating healthier does not mean taking the fun out of eating. It also doesn't mean you have to sacrifice taste to eat healthy. Quite the contrary! Since I met my husband, I have been blown away by the foods that he makes and how he is able to keep it healthy with so much flavor! I am one of those people that "eat to live". I would have never classified myself as a foodie! However, I would now say that I teeter on that foodie fence, when it comes to eating anyway ☺.

Food, Friends & Fun

A mild tangent but trust me, we get back to food! As I mentioned, our youngest daughter was all about that trio, "food, friends & fun". She had an infectious way about her; however, she was not about physical activity like sports. That was a place she and I differed. I've always wanted to participate in a triathlon but it's the long distance running, well... honestly, it's running of any distance, that is just a deal breaker for me. So, for the longest time I put the idea of a triathlon aside.

THEN...one morning I woke up with an epiphany!!! A Foodie Triathlon! Cooking, eating and drinking IS, by (stretching) the definition of a triathlon, "three different events", usually consisting of swimming, cycling, and long-distance running. If truth be told, the foodie triathlon is probably one of the most popular "triathlons'" in everyday living and entertaining. It's just no one ever called it that before! So, as I look back I see that all this time, Sydney had the triathlon mindset and I just needed to catch up.

So, back to rationalizing my triathlon logic. Yes, I knew it would take me some time to "rationalize" this concept, so I got to thinking… there have been pie eating contests, that could be considered a sport, maybe ☺. Then there are cooking shows that have contestants and prizes…that could be called a "sport". So that is two out of three "sports" for our "Foodie Triathlon". But I was stumped on "rationalizing" the final "sport". Thinking long and hard, and while I can't think of any legitimate contests involving alcohol (and there are many good reasons for that!), I realized that the obvious and excellent complement with both eating and cooking is a nice cocktail or glass of wine. It is the perfect tri to my trio. It flows off the tongue even sweeter than "swimming, cycling and long-distance running, don't you agree? ☺

A fun way to use this unique cookbook is to gather a few of your closest friends and create your own "Foodie Triathlon". Pick a few of the recipes within these pages and make both the traditional recipe AND the healthier version and have a "taste off". See if you like the healthier version and maybe even add some of your own tricks to personalize and savor every morsel.

Sizing Up this Book

You will notice three distinct things throughout this book. There are no pictures, there are no greens and there are only a handful of recipes in which you can play. This is intentional. The omission of pictures is to empower you, not compare your creation to someone else's. Everyone's masterpiece will look and taste different. Greens, you might question a book claiming to be "healthier", so why no greens? Salads are pretty simple, throw a bunch of fresh stuff in a bowl with spinach or mixed greens, all organic of course, and add a drizzle of dressing and you're good to go. We wanted to show a few recipes that can still be healthier but lean a little more towards the comfort aspect of the "food taste scale". Everyone loves comfort food, especially when there can be less guilt associated with eating it. And lastly, we purposefully kept this book "bite size" in terms of the number of recipes provided. Looking at a new way of cooking can be overwhelming, so to provide a handful of things to play with versus 100 recipes, keeps things simple and uncomplicated.

So…for our daughter, who was most definitely a 100% foodie, and everyone else that has contributed a recipe in honor of their loved one, let's get cookin'.

the secret ingredient is always love

Sweet Fancy Treats

Maple Bacon Cupcakes

Cupcake Batter

- 1 cup butter, softened
- 1 1/2 cups sugar
- 4 large eggs
- 3 cups all-purpose soft-wheat flour
- 1 tbsp. baking powder
- 1 tsp. salt
- 1 cup milk
- 2 tsp. vanilla extract
- Paper baking cups
- Vegetable cooking spray

Maple Frosting

- 1 cup butter
- 1 (16-oz.) package dark brown sugar
- 1/2 cup evaporated milk
- 1/4 tsp. baking soda
- 1 tbsp. light corn syrup
- 4 cups powdered sugar
- 2 tsp. maple flavoring

Toppings:

- 12 cooked bacon slices, broken to pieces

Directions:

Batter How To's

- Preheat oven to 350 degrees
- Beat butter and sugar at medium speed with an electric mixer until creamy. Add eggs, 1 at a time, beating until blended after each addition
- Combine flour, baking powder, and salt; add to butter mixture alternately with milk, beginning and ending with flour mixture
- Beat at low speed until blended after each addition. Stir in vanilla
- Place paper baking cups in 2 muffin pans
- Coat with cooking spray

- Spoon batter into cups, filling two-thirds full
- Bake for 12-15 minutes or until a wooden pick inserted in center comes out clean
- Cool in pans on wire racks 10 minutes; remove from pans to wire racks
- Cool completely.   Makes 24 cupcakes

Frosting How To's

- To prepare frosting, melt butter in a heavy saucepan over medium heat. Add brown sugar; bring to a boil, stirring constantly
- Stir in evaporated milk, baking soda, and light corn syrup; bring to a boil, stirring occasionally
- Remove from heat, and let cool
- Gradually add powdered sugar; beat at medium speed with an electric mixer until creamy
- Stir in maple flavoring
- Beat at high speed 2 minutes or until creamy. Icing firms up quickly, so use immediately Makes 3 cups
- Top each with bacon pieces

In loving memory of my sister who I miss dearly.
Sydney made these little beauties for my wedding day! Everyone said they were too beautiful to eat (well, almost!). The flavor…well, you will just have to find out for yourself! And wait till you try my Dad's vegan version! Yum
Aubrey Nicole Riegel

Ken's Vegan Maple Bacon Cupcakes

Cupcake Batter

- 3 cups organic All-Purpose Flour
- 1 ½ cups organic Brown Sugar
- 2 tsp. Baking Soda
- ½ tsp. Salt
- 1 ½ Cup water
- 1 Cup unsweetened organic applesauce
- 2 tbsp. White Vinegar
- 1 tsp. Vanilla Extract

Maple Frosting

- ¾ cup vegan butter
- 2 1/3 cup organic powdered sugar
- ¼ tsp. maple extract
- Pinch of Salt
- Tempeh "Bacon"

Cupcake Instructions

- Stir together the flour, brown sugar, baking soda and salt
- Then mix in, the water, applesauce, white vinegar, and vanilla extract
- Fill cupcake liners 3/4 of the way, bake for 20 minutes or until a toothpick draws clean
- Allow to cool completely

Frosting Instructions

- Whip the vegan butter with a mixer on high-speed, and slowly add in the powdered sugar. Add in the maple extract and salt and continue to whip the frosting
- Garnish frosted cupcake with tempeh bacon (see "bacon how to's" on next page)

Tempeh Bacon

- 8 oz. tempeh (250 g)
- 1 tbsp. tamari or soy sauce
- 1 tbsp. extra virgin olive oil for frying the "bacon"
- 1 tbsp. agave syrup
- ½ tsp. red hot sauce
- 2 tsp. liquid smoke or smoke powder
- ½ tsp. ground cumin
- Pinch of salt and ground black pepper

Directions

- Slice the tempeh as thin as you can
- Mix the rest of the ingredients (except the salt) in a bowl. Soak the tempeh slices in the marinade for 1 or 2 minutes
- Heat extra virgin olive oil in a sauté pan and when it's hot, add the tempeh and cook for 1 or 2 minutes each side over high heat until both sides are browned and crisp
- Lay cooked tempeh on paper towel to cool. Add salt to taste

Traditional "Old World" Pastry Dough

- 12 cups pastry flour
- 3 cups lard
- 3 tsp. salt

Directions

- Mix till lard is well worked in
- Add 1 cup (approximately), slowly combine cold water, work till dough sticks together fairly well
- Makes 11-12 crusts, depends on size

Ken's Pastry Dough

- 1 cup almond milk
- 2 1/4 tsp. yeast
- 1 cup granulated sugar
- ½ cup vegan butter
- 2 tsp. salt
- 6 ounces of applesauce
- 4 ½ cups all-purpose flour

Directions

- Combine all ingredients in one bowl and mix by hand, once a dough ball is formed knead for 10 minutes
- Makes three pie crusts

Flourless Chocolate cake

- 12 oz chocolate 72%
- 5 eggs
- 1/3 cup sugar
- 1 cup heavy cream- chilled
- 2 oz espresso
- 10x sugar optional

Directions

- Melt chocolate in Double Boiler stirring occasionally - cool slightly- add espresso
- Combine eggs, and sugar in the mixer and whip until light and ribbon stage
- Turn mixer onto high speed and whip to 3X volume
- Stir 1/4 of the egg mixture into the chocolate mix- fold in remaining egg mix whip cream until med peak, fold into the chocolate mix
- Bake at 350 for 40 minutes in a water bath. Chill overnight and enjoy with a cup of coffee and someone you love
- This cake may also be eaten warm. Be sure to cut with a sharp, warm knife

In loving memory of my mom, Sylvia Horowitz,
who always made life sweeter
Pam Horowitz

Vegan Flourless Chocolate Cake

- 1 cup vegan butter
- 12 oz. vegan 72% chocolate (I like endangered species brand)
- 12 oz. applesauce
- 2/3 cup powdered sugar
- 1/2 cup coconut cream
- 1/4 tsp. baking soda
- 1/2 3/4 cup fresh berries
- 2 oz. espresso if desired
- Powdered sugar, for dusting

Directions

- Preheat the oven to 325. Spray a 6" cake pan and set aside
- Melt chocolate in Double Boiler, add espresso
- Combine applesauce, and sugar in the mixer and whip until light and ribbon stage
- Turn mixer onto high speed and whip to 3X volume
- Once the chocolate and butter are melted, stir sugar until it is dissolved. Fold in cocoa powder and baking soda until a uniform batter is achieved, add the coconut cream
- Stir 1/4 of the applesauce mixture at a time, into the chocolate mix until medium peak
- Transfer batter to prepared cake pan and bake for 35-40 minutes
- Chill overnight
- Dust with powdered sugar and fresh berries to serve

Pound Cake

- 1 lb. butter
- 2 cups sugar
- 7 eggs (add one at a time)
- Pinch of salt
- 1 tsp. baking powder
- 2 1/2 cups flour
- 1 tsp. vanilla

Directions

- Preheat oven to 350. Mix dry ingredients together in a medium sized bowl and set aside
- Beat butter at medium speed with an electric mixer until creamy
- Gradually add sugar, beating at medium speed until light and fluffy. (Butter will turn to a fluffy white.)
- Add eggs, 1 at a time, beating just until yolk disappears
- Add the dry ingredients gradually to creamed butter and sugar
- Beat at low speed just until blended after each addition. (The batter should be smooth)
- Stir in vanilla . Pour into a very well greased and floured 10-inch tube pan
- Bake for 1 hour, insert toothpick in center, done when comes out clean. Cool in pan on a wire rack for 10 to 15 minutes
- Remove from pan, cool completely on a wire rack. Sprinkle with powdered sugar, if desired

In honor of my beloved sister Elizabeth Shack. R. Jade McAuliffe

Vegan Pound Cake

- ½ lb. vegan butter
- 1 cups organic cane sugar
- 12 ounces organic applesauce add in slowly (3 ounces at a time)
- Pinch of salt
- 1 tsp. baking powder
- 2 cups organic flour
- 1 tsp. vanilla

Directions

- Preheat oven to 350
- Mix dry ingredients together in a medium sized bowl and set aside
- Beat butter and sugar at medium speed with an electric mixer until creamy and fluffy
- Add applesauce, 3 ounces at a time, along with a portion of dry mixture beating until it disappears
- Mix in vanilla
- Transfer to greased and floured 10-inch tube pan
- Bake for 1 hour, or until a toothpick inserted in the center comes out clean. Cool completely before serving

Everyday Coffeecake

Batter
- 1 ½ cups flour
- 2 ½ tsp. of baking powder
- ½ tsp. of salt
- 1 egg
- ¾ cup of sugar
- 1/3 cup of butter (melted)
- ½ cup of milk
- 1 tsp. vanilla extract

Crumb Topping
- ½ cup sugar
- ¼ cup flour
- ¼ cup soft butter
- 1 tsp. cinnamon

Directions

- Preheat oven to 375. Grease square pan (8X8 or 9X9)
- Mix batter
- Pour into prepared pan
- Sprinkle with topping mixture
- Bake 25-30 minutes
- For a crumb topping: mix lightly with a fork until crumbly. Sprinkle over batter and bake

Submitted by Ellen Friend in loving memory of my brother, Greg Kearns. Every day during summer break he would make this and eat the entire coffeecake. He would share…sometimes!

Vegan Coffeecake

Cake
- 1 ½ cups organic flour
- 1 ½ tsp. baking powder
- ½ tsp. salt
- 3 oz. cinnamon applesauce
- ¾ cup organic sugar
- 1/3 cup vegan butter
- ½ cup almond milk
- 1 tsp. vanilla extract

Topping
- 4 tbsp. sugar
- 2 tsp. cinnamon
- 2 tbsp. flour
- ¼ cup of vegan butter
- Mix thoroughly with a fork

Directions

- Heat oven to 375
- Mix cake ingredients together to create batter
- Grease pan and pour batter in filling ¾ of the way up
- Sprinkle on topping
- Bake 25-30 minutes

Spicy Chocolate Pie

For the chocolate filling
- 7 oz. dark chocolate, chopped
- 1 cup heavy cream
- 1 egg (at room temperature)
- 1/8 tsp. ground ginger
- 1/8 tsp. cinnamon
- 1/8 tsp. cayenne pepper
- Pinch of salt

For the crust:
- 1 1/2 - 2 cups graham crumbs
- 6-8 tsp. melted butter
- 1/8 tsp. ground ginger
- 1/8 tsp. cinnamon
- 1/8 tsp. cayenne pepper

Directions

- To prepare crust grind graham crackers in a food processor until fine
- Grease a 9-inch pie pan, pour in crumbs, mix in spices, add melted butter in stages, mixing after each addition until the crumbs are the texture of wet mixer
- Firmly press the crumb mixture into the sides of the pan, and along the bottom, forming an even layer. Chill for at least 30 minutes, to prevent the crust from crumbling when cut
- While the crust chills, prepare the chocolate filling. Preheat oven to 350°F. Put chocolate in a large glass bowl
- In a saucepan, heat the heavy cream until it just comes to the boil. Pour over chocolate, and let stand for 1 minute
- Gently whisk the cream and chocolate together until fully combined
- Add egg and whisk in spices and salt
- Pour into chilled piecrust and bake for 25 minutes, or until chocolate filling has puffed up but is still slightly wobbly in the center. Remove from oven and cool completely before topping

Ken's Spicy Vegan Chocolate Pie

- Prepared organic piecrust (or make your own)
- 14 oz. firm drained tofu
- ½ cup chocolate almond milk
- ½ cup peanut butter
- 24 oz. dark chocolate
- Coarse sea salt
- ½ tsp. cayenne pepper
- ½ cup sugar

Directions

- Blend all ingredients except chocolate and salt in blender
- Melt chocolate in a double boiler
- Add melted chocolate to blender ingredients and blend till creamy
- Pour all ingredients into piecrust
- Sprinkle coarse salt as desired on top and chill for 12 hours
  NOTE: You can purchase premade organic piecrust

Sugar Cookies

- 3 cup all-purpose flour, plus more for surface
- 1 tsp. baking powder
- ½ tsp. salt
- 1 cup butter, softened
- 1 cup granulated sugar
- 1 large egg
- 1 tsp. pure vanilla extract
- 1 tbsp. milk

Directions

- In a large bowl, whisk together flour, baking powder, and salt and set aside
- In another large bowl, beat butter and sugar until fluffy and pale in color. Add egg, milk, and vanilla and beat until combined, then add flour mixture gradually until totally combined
- Shape into a disk and wrap in plastic. Refrigerate 1 hour
- When ready to roll, preheat oven to 350° and line two baking sheets with parchment paper. Lightly flour a clean work surface and roll out dough until 1/8" thick. Cut out shapes and transfer to prepared baking sheets

Ken's Sugar Cookies

- ½ cup vegan butter (such as Earth Balance)
- ½ cup organic cane sugar
- ¼ cup organic brown sugar
- ¼ cup organic applesauce
- 1 tsp. pure vanilla extract
- 1 ¾ cups organic all-purpose flour
- 1 tsp. baking powder
- ½ tsp. baking soda
- ¼ tsp. salt
- 1-2 tsp. soy or almond milk

Directions

- Preheat oven 350 degrees
- Make ½ inch to 1 inch balls and place on cookie sheet
- Bake 10-12 minutes

Buckeye's

- 1 ½ cups peanut butter
- 1 cup butter, softened
- ½ tsp. vanilla extract
- 6 cups confectioners' sugar
- 4 cups semisweet chocolate chips

Directions

- In a large bowl, mix together the peanut butter, butter, vanilla and confectioners' sugar. The dough will look dry
- Roll into 1 inch balls and place on a waxed paper-lined cookie sheet
- Press a toothpick into the top of each ball to be used later as the handle for dipping
- Chill in freezer until firm, about 30 minutes
- Melt chocolate chips in a double boiler or in a bowl set over a pan of barely simmering water. Stir frequently until smooth
- Dip frozen peanut butter balls in chocolate holding onto the toothpick. Leave a small portion of peanut butter showing at the top to make them look like Buckeyes
- Put back on the cookie sheet and refrigerate until serving

Vegan Buckeye's

- 1 ib. organic powdered sugar
- 2 ib. organic peanut butter
- ½ ib. vegan butter
- 2 - 12 oz. bags vegan chocolate chips

Directions

- In a large bowl, mix together the peanut butter, organic powered sugar and vegan butter
- Roll into 1 inch balls and place on a waxed paper-lined cookie sheet
- Press a toothpick into the top of each ball to be used later as the handle for dipping
- Chill in fridge until firm, about 30 minutes
- Melt vegan chocolate chips in a double boiler or in a bowl set over a pan of barely simmering water. Stir frequently until smooth
- Dip chilled peanut butter balls in chocolate holding onto the toothpick. Leave a small portion of peanut butter showing at the top to make them look like Buckeyes
- Put back in refrigerator in Tupperware with wax paper dividing rows until served
- This will yield 126 Buckeyes

Blueberry Muffins

- 2 cups all purpose flour
- ¾ cup granulated sugar
- 2 tsp. baking powder
- 1/4 tsp. Salt
- 1 cup Milk
- 2 large eggs
- 1 tsp. vanilla extract
- ½ cup butter, melted and cooled slightly (1 Stick)
- 2 cups blueberries (Fresh or Frozen)

Directions

- Preheat oven to 375 degrees. Prepare a 12 cup muffin pan with non-stick cooking spray or paper liners, and set aside
- In a large bowl, whisk together the flour, sugar, baking powder, and salt
- In another bowl, whisk together the milk, eggs, vanilla extract, and melted butter
- Pour the wet ingredients into the dry ingredients and mix gently just until combined, being careful not to over mix
- Gently fold the blueberries into the batter
- Fill the muffin cups up to the top with batter
- Bake in preheated oven for 15-20 minutes, until slightly golden brown on the top and a toothpick inserted in the center of the muffins comes out clean

Ken's Vegan Blueberry Muffins

Muffin batter
- 1 ½ cups organic all-purpose flour
- ¾ cup organic white sugar
- ½ tsp. salt
- 2 tsp. baking powder
- 1/3 cup canola oil
- 3 oz. organic cinnamon applesauce
- 1/3 cup soy or almond milk
- 2 cups fresh blueberries

Crumb Topping
- ½ cup organic white sugar
- 1/3 cup organic all-purpose flour
- ¼ cup earth balance
- 1 ½ tsp. ground cinnamon

Directions

- Preheat oven to 400 degrees. Line pan with muffin liners
- Combine all ingredients and mix well then add in blueberries. Fill muffin cups and sprinkle with crumb topping mixture
- To Make crumb topping mix all ingredients together with a fork, and sprinkle over muffins before baking
- Bake for 20 to 25 minutes in the preheated oven, or until done

Cinnamon Rolls

Dough
- 1 package (1/4 ounce) active dry yeast
- 1 cup warm whole milk (110° to 115°)
- ½ cup sugar
- 1/3 cup butter, melted
- 2 large eggs, room temperature
- 1 tsp. salt
- 4 to 4 ½ cups all-purpose flour

Filling
- ¾ cup packed brown sugar
- 2 tbsp. ground cinnamon
- ¼ cup butter, melted

Frosting
- ½ cup butter, softened
- ¼ cup cream cheese, softened
- ½ tsp. vanilla extract
- 1/8 tsp. salt
- 1-1/2 cups confectioners' sugar

Directions

- Dissolve yeast in warm milk. In another bowl, combine sugar, butter, eggs, salt, yeast mixture and 2 cups flour; beat on medium speed until smooth
- Stir in enough remaining flour to form a soft dough (dough will be sticky)
- Turn dough onto a floured surface; knead until smooth and elastic, 6-8 minutes. Place in a greased bowl, turning once to grease the top. Cover and let rise in a warm place until doubled, about 1 hour
- Mix brown sugar and cinnamon. Punch down dough; divide in half. On a lightly floured surface, roll one portion into an 11x8-in. rectangle

- Brush with 2 tablespoons butter; sprinkle with half of the brown sugar mixture to within 1/2 in. of edges. Roll up jelly-roll style, starting with a long side; pinch seam to seal
- Cut into eight slices; place in a greased 13x9-in. pan, cut side down. Cover with a **kitchen towel. Repeat with** remaining dough and filling. Let rise in a warm place until doubled, about 1 hour
- Preheat oven to 350°
- Bake until golden brown, 20-25 minutes. Cool on wire racks
- For frosting, beat butter, cream cheese, vanilla and salt until blended; gradually beat in confectioners' sugar. Spread over tops. Refrigerate leftovers

Ken's Vegan Cinnamon Roll's

Dough
- 4 ½ cups organic all-purpose flour
- 2 ¼ tsp. yeast
- ½ cup organic granulated sugar
- ½ cup vegan butter
- 6 ounces of organic cinnamon applesauce
- 2 tsp. salt
- 1 cup almond milk

Filling (Double this)
- 2 cup organic packed brown sugar
- 5 tbsp. cinnamon
- ¼ cup vegan butter

Icing
- 1/2 cup vegan butter softened
- 1/8 tsp. salt
- ¼ cup kite hill cream cheese
- ½ tbsp. vanilla
- 1 ½ cup powdered sugar

Directions

Dough:

- Add yeast and sugar to warm milk in a large bowl. Stir gently to combine. Stir in melted butter, salt, applesauce, and flour into yeast mixture. Gently mix until well-combined
- Knead dough 10 minutes and then place into a large greased glass bowl. Cover lightly with plastic and place in a warm location. Allow the dough to double in size

Filling:

- Roll out dough to a 1/4 inch thickness
- Stir together the brown sugar and cinnamon and sprinkle generously all over the dough.
- Tightly roll the dough, until a log of dough has been formed

- Cut the dough into 1-inch slices and place onto a lightly greased sheet pan

Baking

- Preheat oven to 400°
- Allow rolls to rise for 30 minutes on sheet pan
- Place rolls into oven and cook til lightly browned and but not overcooked, about 15 minutes

Icing

- Combine vegan butter, powdered sugar, cream cheese, vanilla and salt
- Whip until consistency desired
- Spread frosting generously over rolls while they are warm

Pizzelle's

- 12 eggs
- 2 tsp. Anise
- 1 cup Mazola oil
- 1 cup Crisco oil
- 8 cups flour
- 4 tsp. baking powder
- ¼ tsp. salt
- 4 cups sugar
- ¼ cup whiskey

Directions

- Cream, oil, Crisco, sugar, add eggs, beat till creamy
- Add whiskey and anise
- Combine dry ingredients
- Add to wet

Is this is how I received my recipes. They knew how to do everything by eye, touch, feel. You drop them on the iron by tablespoon. I loved holidays in our home – truly. It was magical and every holiday had certain recipes. I love this because my nanny, mom and I would sit for hours making these (while everyone was sleeping) and talk and laugh. I also loved when my nanny made the "old fashioned" pizzelle with the pizzelle irons on the stove. I would roll the balls of dough and she would have two irons going, flipping & turning. The smell was amazing and we would have stacks of pizzelle. We would pack and wrap them for family & friends ❤

In memory of Rose Amabile & Rita Bentivoglio
By Christine Bentivoglio Worstall

Vegan Pizzelle's

- ½ cup vegan butter melted and cool
- 1 cup organic sugar
- ½ cup almond milk
- ½ tsp. vanilla
- ½ tsp. anise
- 1 tsp. orange juice
- 1 ¾ cups flour
- 1 ¾ tsp. baking powder

Directions:

- Blend together vegan butter, sugar and almond milk
- Add vanilla, anise and orange juice
- Whisk together flour and baking powder
- Using a mixer, gradually add flour mixture to liquid mixture. Should be like cream puff dough
- Heat pizzelle maker according to directions
- Bake 30 seconds or till lightly browned
- Place flat on plate or cookie sheet
- Makes 30 pizzelle

Salted Chocolate Chip Cookies

- 1 ¾ cups all-purpose flour
- 1 ¼ tsp. baking soda
- 1 tsp. baking powder
- ¾ cup light brown sugar, packed
- ½ cup granulated sugar
- ½ tsp. salt
- 2 large eggs
- ½ cup unsalted butter, softened
- 1 ½ tsp. vanilla extract
- 8 ounces bittersweet chocolate, coarsely chopped
- Flaky sea salt

Directions

- Preheat oven to 450°
- Whisk together flour, baking soda, baking powder, and salt
- Beat butter and sugars with a mixer at medium speed, 2-3 minutes
- Add eggs and vanilla; beat until pale, 4-5 minutes. Reduce mixer speed to low and gradually add flour mixture until just blended
- Fold in chocolate chunks using a rubber spatula
- Using a spoon, scoop dough into even portions, place on baking sheets
- Sprinkle cookies with flaky salt and refrigerate sheets until dough is firm to touch, 10 minutes
- Bake for 6-7 minutes
- Let cool on baking sheets for 5 minutes

Ken's Vegan Salted Chocolate Chip Cookies

- 2 cups organic all-purpose flour
- 1 tsp. baking powder
- ¾ tsp. baking soda
- ½ tsp. fine salt
- 1 ¼ cups dark chocolate chips
- ½ cup organic sugar
- ½ cup packed light or dark brown sugar
- ½ cup canola oil
- ¼ cup water
- Coarse-grained sea salt

Directions

- In a large bowl, whisk together flour, baking powder, baking soda, and salt. Add the chocolate chips to the flour mixture and toss
- In a separate large bowl, mix the sugars with the canola oil and water until smooth and incorporated
- Add the flour mixture to the sugar mixture, and then stir until combined
- Cover with plastic wrap. Refrigerate the dough 12 hours to 24 hours
- Remove dough and portion into 2-inch mounds
- Sprinkle the balls of dough with coarse-grained sea salt
- Bake for 12 to 13 minutes, or until the edges are just golden

Cornbread Muffins

- 1 ¼ cups yellow, white or blue cornmeal
- 1 cup all-purpose flour
- ½ cup granulated sugar
- 1 tbsp. baking powder
- ½ tsp. salt
- ¼ cup butter
- 1 cup milk
- 1 large egg

Directions

- Spray the bottom and sides of an 8-inch square pan or 9-inch round cake pan with the cooking spray
- In a 1-quart saucepan, heat the butter over low heat until melted
- In a large bowl, beat the melted butter, milk and egg with a fork or wire whisk until well mixed
- Add the cornmeal, flour, sugar, baking powder and salt all at once; stir just until the flour is moistened (batter will be lumpy)
- Pour batter into the pan; use a rubber spatula to scrape batter from bowl. Spread batter evenly in pan and smooth top of batter
- Bake 20 to 25 minutes or until golden brown and a toothpick inserted in the center comes out clean
- Heat the oven to 400

Ken's Vegan Cornbread Muffins

- 1 cup organic all-purpose flour
- 1 ½ cup organic yellow cornmeal
- ½ bag frozen organic corn
- ¼ cup organic sugar
- 1 ½ tsp. baking powder
- ¼ tsp. baking soda
- ½ tsp. salt
- 4 oz. organic applesauce
- ½ cup almond milk
- ½ cup vegan butter

Directions

- Preheat oven at 350
- Mix all ingredients in a blender till smooth but slightly gritty
- Bake for 25 to 30 minutes
- Finished when you insert toothpick in center and it comes out clean

Peach Kuchen

- 2 cup sifted flour
- 1/4 tsp. baking powder
- 1/2 tsp. salt
- 1 cup sugar
- 1/2 cup butter
- 12 peaches, peeled & sliced
- 1 tsp. cinnamon
- 2 egg yolks
- 1 cup heavy cream

Directions

- Preheat oven to 400
- Sift flour, baking powder, salt & 2 tbsp. of sugar together
- Work in butter with 2 knives or pastry cutter until mixture looks like meal
- Pile evenly in 2, 9 inch pie dishes. Pat even layer over bottom and sides
- Place peach slices over pastry and sprinkle with sugar and cinnamon
- Place in oven for 15 minutes
- Mix egg yolks and heavy cream together and pour over peaches
- Reduce oven to 325 degrees
- Return pies to oven for 20-30 minutes
- Serve warm. Makes 2, 9 inch pies

In loving memory of my son Jamie.
Forever your Ma (Joanne Braunsberg)

Vegan Peach Kuchen

- 2 cup sifted organic all-purpose flour
- ¼ tsp. baking powder
- ½ tsp. salt
- 1 cup organic sugar
- ½ cup vegan butter
- 12 peaches, peeled & sliced
- 1 tsp. cinnamon
- 6 oz. organic applesauce
- 1 cup coconut cream

Directions

- Preheat oven to 400 degrees
- Sift flour, baking powder, salt & 2 tbsp. of sugar together
- Work in butter with 2 knives or pastry cutter until mixture looks like meal
- Pile evenly in 2, 9 inch pie dishes. Pat even layer over bottom and sides
- Place peach slices over pastry and sprinkle with sugar and cinnamon
- Place in oven for 15 minutes
- Mix applesauce and coconut cream together and pour over peaches
- Reduce oven to 325 degrees
- Return pies to oven for 20-30 minutes
- Serve warm. Makes 2, 9 inch pies

Chocolate Cake

- 2 cups sugar
- 1 ¾ cups flour
- ¾ cup cocoa powder
- 1 ½ tsp. baking powder
- 2 tsp. baking soda
- ½ tsp. salt
- 2 eggs
- 1 cup milk
- ½ cup vegetable oil
- 1 tsp. vanilla extract
- 1 cup boiling water

Directions

- Preheat oven to 350
- Grease and flour your baking pan or line your muffin pan with paper liners for cupcakes
- In a large bowl, combine sugar, flour, cocoa, baking powder, baking soda and salt in large bowl
- Add eggs, milk, oil and vanilla to dry mixture and mix with an electric mixer on medium for about 2 minutes
- Gently mix in boiling water
- Pour into pans and bake
- Cool on wire racks

Ken's Vegan Chocolate Cake

- 1 ½ cups organic pastry flour
- 1/3 cup unsweetened cocoa powder
- 1 tsp. baking soda
- ½ tsp. salt
- 1 cup organic sugar
- ½ cup canola oil
- 2 tsp. vanilla extract
- 1 cup cold water
- 2 tbsp. white vinegar

Directions

- Preheat oven to 350
- Mix all ingredients in one bow except for the vinegar
- Once all ingredients are mixed thoroughly add the vinegar and mix briskly…you will notice a change in color of the batter
- Place in oven for 25 minutes or until toothpick pulls out clean
- Use either powdered sugar sifted over the cake or icing after cooling for an hour

"Drinks pair nicely with good food and amazing friends"

Libations

Sydney Lou Who

- 2 part Ruby Red grapefruit juice
- 3 parts St. Germaine
- 1 tbsp. sugar
- 1 tbsp. ground cinnamon
- Lemon juice
- Orange or grapefruit wedge as garnish

Directions

- Chill a martini glass
- Mix the cranberry and St. Germaine in a mixer with ice and shake
- Pour a few drops of lemon juice into a shot glass and wipe the rim of the martini glass
- On a small plate, combine sugar and cinnamon
- Place the rim of the martini glass, with the lemon juice already on the rim, into the cinnamon sugar mixer and turn to ensure even placement around the glass
- Pour the contents into the chilled glass
- Garnish with an orange or grapefruit wedge

Ken's Cosmo

- 4 parts cranberry
- 1 part vodka
- 1 part Cointreau
- 1 part Rose's Lime Juice

Directions

- Chill a martini glass
- Mix the cranberry, vodka, Cointreau and lime juice in a mixer with ice and shake
- Pour the contents into the chilled glass

Apple Cider Mimosa

- 2 tbsp. sugar
- 1 tbsp. ground cinnamon
- 1 cup apple cider
- 1 bottle sparkling wine
- Cinnamon sticks

Directions

- On a small plate, combine sugar and cinnamon
- Dip champagne flutes in water to wet the rims, then dip in cinnamon sugar mixture
- Fill champagne flutes 1/4 full with apple cider, then top off with sparkling wine
- Garnish with a cinnamon stick

Pina Colada

- 1 ½ cup ice
- ½ cup diced pineapple, frozen
- 2 oz. pineapple juice
- 2 oz. coconut cream
- 1 ½ oz. white rum
- 1 oz. dark rum
- Pineapple slices

Directions

- Put the ice, frozen pineapple, juice, coconut cream, and the white and dark rums into a blender
- Blend until smooth and frosty
- Pour the drink into 2 glasses
- Garnish the rim with pineapple slices

Giddy Geisha

- 3 ounces Vodka
- 2 ounce pomegranate juice
- 1/2 ounce rose water**
- Sparkling wine*
- Lime wedge for garnish

Directions

- Fill a shaker with ice and ingredients and shake
- Strain the contents of the shaker into the glass
- Add sparkling wine, lighter for a heavier taste and more for a lighter taste
- Squeeze a lime wedge in the drink
- Garnish with an additional lime wedge

**Rose water is available on Amazon and at natural, international & specialty food markets

Bomb a'grante

- ½ parts St. Germaine
- 2 parts vodka
- ½ part fig
- 1 oz. lemon juice
- ½ agave
- 1 part pomegranate juice

Directions

- Chill a snifter
- Combine and mix in a shaker with ice and shake
- Pour the contents into chilled snifter with ice

Peachy Keen

- 3 parts cranberry juice
- 1 part peach schnapps
- 1 part vodka

Directions

- Chill a martini glass
- Combine and mix in a shaker with ice and shake
- Pour the contents into chilled glass

Mint Hot Chocolate

- 3 cups organic coconut milk
- ½ cup organic raw cocoa powder
- ½ cup organic cane sugar
- 1/8 tsp. of salt
- 1 tsp. vanilla extract
- 2 or more shots of Crème de Menthe

Directions

- Mix all ingredients except for Creme de Menthe and vanilla in a large pot and bring to a simmer
- Add vanilla and crème de menthe
- Mix well and serve hot
- You can substitute raw cocoa powder for a vegan dark chocolate and melt it in a double boiler

Sweet n' Sour Gummy Bear

- 3 parts Kinky Blue Liqueur
- 2 parts Sparkling Wine
- Sugar (optional)
- 2 parts Rose's Lime Juice
- Lime for garnish

Directions

- Chill glass
- Fill a shaker with ice and Kinky Blue and Rose's lime juice and shake
- Strain the contents of the shaker into the glass
- Add sparkling wine
- Rub the lime wedge around the edge of glass and dip in the sugar
- Garnish with an additional lime wedge

Italian Ice

- 3 cups Sparking Wine, chilled
- 1 cup Limoncello liqueur, chilled
- 1 cup frozen raspberries
- 6 sprigs fresh mint

Directions

- In a large pitcher, whisk together Sparking Wine and Limoncello
- Serve over raspberries, garnished with mint, if desired

GREAT FRIENDS

GREAT GOOD

GREAT TIMES

Munchies

Spinach & Artichoke Dip

- 2 cup shredded parmesan cheese
- 10 oz. box frozen chopped spinach thawed
- 14 oz. can artichoke hearts drained and chopped
- 2 tsp. minced garlic
- 2/3 cup sour cream
- 8 oz. cream cheese softened
- 1/3 cup mayonnaise
- Pita chips or cut veggies

Directions

- Preheat oven to 375
- Mix together Parmesan cheese, spinach and artichoke hearts
- In a separate bowl, mix together sour cream, cream cheese, mayo and garlic
- Add to spinach mixture and mix until well combined
- Pour into a baking dish
- Bake for 25 minutes
- Serve warm with veggies or pita chips

Ken's Vegan Spinach Artichoke Dip

- 2 tbsp. olive oil
- 1 onion finely chopped
- 3 cloves garlic Minced
- ½ teaspoon of pepper flakes
- 5 oz. baby spinach
- 14 once of soft tofu drained
- ½ cup nutritional yeast
- 2 tbsp. lemon juice
- 1 tsp. dried basil
- 1 ½ tsp. of salt
- ½ tsp. black pepper
- 14 oz. artichoke hearts
- Tortilla chips or cut veggies

Directions

- Preheat oven to 350
- Grease 1 quart baking dish in olive oil
- Sauté onions until soft, add garlic and red pepper and cook for 5 minutes on medium heat
- Reduce heat to low and add spinach and cook till wilted
- In a food processor blend tofu, nutritional yeast, lemon juice, basil, salt, pepper until smooth, then add artichokes and spinach mixture and pulse till chunky
- Place in baking dish
- Bake for 30 minutes

Pierogies

Filling
4 medium potatoes, peeled and cubed
2 medium onions, chopped
2 tbsp. butter
5 oz. cream cheese, softened
1/2 tsp. salt
1/2 tsp. pepper

Dough
5 cups all-purpose flour
1 tsp. salt
1 cup water
3 large eggs
1/2 cup butter, softened

Directions

- In a food processor, combine flour and salt; cover and pulse to blend
- Add water, eggs and butter; cover and pulse until dough forms a ball, adding an additional 1 to 2 tablespoons of water or flour if needed
- Let rest, covered, 15 to 30 minutes
- Place potatoes in a large saucepan and cover with water
- Bring to a boil over high heat. Reduce heat; cover and simmer 10-15 minutes or until tender
- Meanwhile, in a large skillet over medium-high heat, sauté onions in butter until tender; set aside
- Drain potatoes. Over very low heat, stir potatoes for 1-2 minutes or until steam has evaporated
- Press through a potato ricer or strainer into a large bowl. Stir in cream cheese, salt, pepper and onion mixture; set aside
- Divide dough into four parts

- On a lightly floured surface, roll one portion of dough to 1/8-in. thickness; cut with a floured 3-in. round cookie cutter
- Place 2 teaspoons of filling in center of each circle. Moisten edges with water; fold in half and press edges to seal
- Repeat with remaining dough and filling
- Bring a Dutch oven of water to a boil over high heat; add pierogies in batches
- Reduce heat to a gentle simmer; cook for 1-2 minutes or until pierogies float to the top and are tender
- Remove with a slotted spoon
- In a large skillet, sauté four pierogies and onion in butter until pierogies are lightly browned and heated through; sprinkle with parsley

Ken's Vegan Pierogies

Filling

- 1 ½ tbsp. salt
- 1 tbsp. garlic powder
- 1 tbsp. pepper
- 1 cup almond milk
- 6 pounds potatoes (quartered)
- 3 containers Kite Hill ricotta cheese
- ½ cup earth balance
- 2 bunches scallions finely chopped

Dough

- Durum wheat
- Water

Directions

Filling

- Steam potatoes
- Put in bowl, mash with hand masher, add all other ingredients and mix well but don't cream. Consistency of chunky mashed potatoes

Dough

- Mix together and knead for 10 minutes
- Roll out to 1/8-1/4 inch thick
- Cut 4 inch circles
- 1 large tablespoon of potato mixture per pierogi
- Fold dough in half circle

- Use a fork to press the ends together to seal the pierogi

Cooking options
- Steam
- Fry in 1 tbsp. of oil

- If you refrigerate, place between layers of wax paper so they do not stick together. Must be used within 2 -3 days
- Freeze option: Place cooled pierogies on waxed paper-lined baking or cookie pan; freeze until firm. Transfer to resealable plastic freezer bags; freeze up to 3 months

Poor Man's Pizza (Greg's Pizza)

- White bread (Stroehman's or store brand)
- Ketchup
- Kraft parmesan cheese (100% grated in the container)
- Italian seasoning

Directions

- Place bread on a cookie sheet
- Spread each piece with ketchup and sprinkle cheese and seasonings
- Broil in toaster oven or regular oven until toasted

In loving memory of my brother Greg.
Ellen Friend

Ken's Vegan Mushroom Truffle Pizza

- Pizza crust*
- Salt
- Pepper
- Garlic cloves (chopped)
- Garlic powder
- Onion powder
- Pepper flakes
- Truffle oil
- Organic mushrooms
- ½ pkg. Daiya mozzarella shredded cheese

Directions

- Heat oven to 400
- Place cheese in bowl and sprinkle garlic powder, onion powder, salt, pepper and pepper flakes over it and mix
- Place mushrooms in a pan add some water and begin to steam them along with 1 tablespoon of chopped garlic. When mushrooms are cooked, drain but leave garlic bits in with mushrooms
- One the pizza dough sprinkle some truffle oil
- Place the mushroom/garlic mixture evenly around the dough
- Sprinkle on the cheese mixture evenly around the dough
- Finish off with additional truffle oil splashed on the top
- Bake for 12 minutes or until done the way you like it (crispy, doughy etc)
- *Pizza crust (Organic premade or make your own using only durum wheat and water)

Nachos

- 5 oz. tortilla chips
- 1 cup shredded cheddar cheese
- 1 cup cooked chicken cubed
- 1/3 cup corn
- 1/3 cup black beans
- 1 4 oz. can diced green chiles
- 1/3 cup diced red onion
- 1/4 cup diced tomatoes
- 1/4 cup crumbled feta cheese

Toppings
- Diced avocado
- Sour cream or Greek yogurt
- Slices Jalapeño

Directions

- Turn the broiler on low
- Spread the tortilla chips out evenly onto a large baking sheet
- Sprinkle tortillas chips evenly with shredded cheddar cheese
- Place the sheet in the oven under the broiler until the cheese is melted, about 45 seconds to a minute
- Remove the baking sheet from oven and top the tortilla chips with chicken, corn, black beans, green chilies, tomatoes and feta
- Return the baking sheet to the oven under the broiler for another 30 to 45 seconds
- Top the nachos with some diced avocado, sour cream and jalapeño slices

Ken's Vegan Nachos

- Use cheddar cheese recipe*
- 1 bag favorite tortilla chips
- 1 can of sliced black olives
- 1 bunch scallions chopped
- Salt & pepper to taste
- 3 jalapeno peppers chopped
- 1 can black beans
- 2 cups of organic sweet corn
- 1 ½ cups diced tomatoes

Directions

- If making cheddar sauce follow directions below and pour over nachos
- If using shredded vegan cheddar cheese place over nachos once prepared
- Nachos
- In a large baking tray place a bag of chips and evenly spread them out
- Place all your ingredient on and throughout chips
- Add any version of the cheese
- Bake for 15 minutes on 350

Cheddar Cheese

- Mix 1 cup soy milk and one tablespoon of vegan butter and one teaspoon of pepper
- Bring the liquid to a simmer and then Combine one package of Daiya shredded cheddar
- Once melted remove cheese from pot and place in blender to cream it

Quesadilla's

- 1 tbsp. butter
- 4 flour tortillas (8 inches)
- 2 ounces cream cheese, softened
- ¼ cup shredded sharp cheddar cheese
- ¼ cup shredded Monterey Jack cheese
- 2 tbsp. thinly sliced green onion
- 2 tsp. chopped ripe olives
- ¼ cup salsa
- Salt & pepper to taste
- Sour cream, optional

Directions

- Butter one side of each tortilla
- Spread cream cheese over unbuttered side on half the tortillas
- Sprinkle with cheeses, onion and olives. Top with remaining tortillas, buttered side up
- Cook on a panini pan over medium heat for 1-2 minutes on each side or until cheese is melted. Cut into wedges
- Optional – use salt, pepper and serve with salsa and sour cream

Ken's Vegan Quesadilla's

- 2 quesadilla wrappers
- 1 package organic mushrooms
- 3 minced cloves of Garlic
- Mozzarella cheese shreds (Daiya)
- 1 onion
- 1 can refried beans
- Red pepper flakes
- Salt

Directions

- Cook garlic for 5 minutes in 5 tablespoons of water medium heat
- Add mushrooms and cook till tender (ad more water if needed)
- On bottom shell spread refried beans
- Slice onion thinly and place across beans
- Drain mushrooms but leave garlic in
- Spread mushrooms across beans
- Layer cheese on next
- Cover with top shell
- Bake 20 minutes at 350

"All food provides comfort when it's made with love"

Satisfying Sides
Soups
Stuffin's & Sauces

Mac and Cheese

- 2 cups milk
- 2 tbsp. butter
- 2 tbsp. all-purpose flour
- 1/2 tsp. salt
- 1/4 tsp. freshly ground black pepper
- 1 (10-oz.) block extra sharp Cheddar cheese, shredded
- 1/2 (16-oz.) package elbow macaroni, cooked

Directions

- Preheat oven to 400 degrees
- Heat milk at HIGH for 1 1/2 minutes
- Melt butter in a large skillet over medium-low heat; whisk in flour until smooth. Cook, whisking constantly, 1 minute
- Gradually whisk in warm milk, and cook, whisking constantly, 5 minutes or until thickened
- Blend in salt, black pepper, 1 cup shredded cheese until smooth; stir in pasta. Spoon pasta mixture into a lightly greased 2-qt. baking dish; top with remaining cheese
- Bake at 400° for 20 minutes or until golden

Ken's Vegan Mac and Cheese

- 1/3 cup earth balance
- 1 tsp. salt
- ½ tsp. pepper
- 1 cup coconut or almond unsweetened milk
- 1½ bags of Daiya cheddar cheese shreds
- 1 bag of pasta (your choice)

Directions

- Cook pasta as directed…set aside
- Heat all ingredients except for cheese
- Bring to a light boil
- Slowly add cheese constantly stirring
- Once cheese is melted but lumpy transfer to a Vitamix or blender and blend until creamy
- Mix cheese and past together, top with red pepper flakes to your liking

Option
Sprinkle organic vegan breadcrumbs and bake at 350 for 20 minutes or until golden brown

Scalloped Potatoes

- 2 tbsp. butter
- 1 tsp. salt
- ¼ tsp. pepper
- 3 tbsp. all-purpose flour
- 1 ½ cups milk
- ½ cup shredded cheddar cheese
- 1 cup thinly sliced onions, divided
- 2 pounds red potatoes, peeled and thinly sliced (about 4 cups)

Directions

- Preheat oven to 350 degrees
- In a small saucepan, melt butter; stir in flour, salt and pepper until smooth
- Gradually whisk in milk
- Bring to a boil, stirring constantly; cook and stir until thickened, about 2 minutes
- Remove from heat; stir in cheese until melted
- Coat an 8-in. square baking dish with cooking spray
- Place half of the potatoes in dish; layer with ½ cup onion and half of the cheese sauce. Repeat layers
- Bake, covered, 50 minutes
- Uncover; bake until bubbly and potatoes are tender, 10-15 minutes longer

Ken's Vegan Scalloped Potatoes

- 3 pounds potatoes sliced thinly
- 1 onion thinly sliced
- 2 bags Daiya mozzarella cheese shreds
- 6 tbsp. vegan butter
- 1 tsp. salt
- 1 tsp. pepper
- 2 cups unsweetened almond milk

Directions

- Preheat oven to 375 degrees. Grease a 8 x 8 inch baking dish
- Bring milk butter and seasoning to a light boil in a 2 quart pot
- Add in cheese and mix. For a creamier consistency take those ingredients once melted and place in a blender to cream
- Spread 1/4 of the potato slices into the bottom of the prepared baking dish. Top with about 1/4 of the onion slices. Pour 1/4 of the cheese mixture over the potato and onion
- Repeat layering
- Bake in oven 60 minutes

Green Bean Almondine

- 2 9 oz. frozen green beans
- 2 tbsp. slivered almonds
- 2 tbsp. butter
- 1 tsp. lemon juice

Directions

- Cook green beans covered in a small amount of boiling salted water until crisp-tender
- Drain and pat dry
- Cook almonds in butter over low heat, stirring occasionally, until golden
- Remove from heat and add juice
- Pour over beans

Vegan Green Bean Almondine

- 1 tbsp. olive oil
- 1 tbsp. vegan butter
- 2 tbsp. minced shallot
- Juice from 1 lemon (about ¼ cup)
- 1 ½ lb. fresh green beans
- ¼ cup sliced almonds
- Pinch sea salt
- Pinch cracked black pepper

Directions

- Place trimmed green beans in a large skillet. Add a pinch of salt and enough water to just cover green beans
- Boil for 3-4 minutes, or until beans are bright green
- Drain and place green beans in an ice bath to stop the cooking process
- Heat oven to 400 degrees. Place almonds in a single layer on a baking sheet lined with aluminum foil and toast about 5 minutes or until lightly golden, careful not to burn. Remove from oven
- Using the same skillet as the green beans, melt vegan butter and olive oil over low heat
- Add shallot, salt and pepper to taste. Add lemon juice and continue cooking, stirring, until slightly thickened
- Add beans back into skillet and cook until beans are warmed through, 7-10 minutes
- Remove from pan and arrange on a serving dish. Top with toasted almonds
- NOTE: For softer green beans, cook them a bit longer and sauce can made a day in advance kept refrigerated

Mashed Potatoes

- 3 medium baking potatoes peeled and coarsely chopped
- 1 tsp. salt
- 4 tbsp. butter, room temperature
- 1/4 cup sour cream, room temperature
- 1 tsp. finely minced garlic
- 1 tbsp. whole milk, room temperature
- Salt and freshly ground black pepper

Directions

- In a medium saucepan, cook the potatoes in salted water until tender, about 15 minutes
- Drain the potatoes and return them to the saucepan
- Add the butter, sour cream and garlic
- Mash the potatoes with a potato masher or the back of a fork until the ingredients are blended
- Add the milk, 1 tablespoon at a time, until the potatoes are the desired consistency
- Taste and add salt and pepper, if needed

Ken's Vegan Mashed Potatoes

- 4 large potatoes
- 1 jar organic garlic, chopped
- 1 tsp. olive oil
- 4 tbsp. vegan butter
- 1/4-1/2 cup (60-120ml) soy or almond milk
- Sea salt and black pepper to taste

Directions

- Peel and slice the potatoes into halves and then slice each half into quarters. Place the potatoes into a pot and cover with water
- Bring to the boil and cook covered for around 20-25 minutes until soft
- When the potatoes are cooked, drain the water from the pot and leave the potatoes behind in the pot and allow them to sit for a few minutes to drain
- Then add the vegan butter and mash in with a potato masher
- Then add the milk, starting with 1/4 cup and mashing it in, if it still looks a little dry, add another 1/4 cup of soy or almond milk
- Add sea salt and black pepper to taste

Butternut Squash Soup

- 2 carrots, cut into 1-inch pieces
- 1 sweet onion, chopped
- 3 tbsp. olive oil
- 1 (3-lb.) butternut squash, peeled and cut into cubes
- 6 cups chicken broth
- 1 tsp. orange zest
- 3 tbsp. white wine vinegar
- 1 tbsp. honey
- ¾ tsp. kosher salt
- ½ tsp. freshly ground white pepper
- ½ tsp. hot sauce
- Garnish: bacon pieces

Directions

- Sauté carrots and onion in hot olive oil in a covered pot over medium-high heat 8 to 10 minutes or until lightly browned
- Add squash, broth, and orange zest; bring to a boil
- Cover, reduce heat to medium, and simmer 20 to 25 minutes or until squash is tender
- Stir in cream, vinegar, honey, salt, white pepper and hot sauce. Cool slightly (about 10 minutes)
- Process mixture with a blender until smooth
- Serve warm

Ken's Vegan Butternut Squash Soup

- 2 tbsp. vegan butter
- 1 onion chopped
- 1 celery stalk chopped
- 1 carrot chopped
- 2 potatoes chopped
- 1 butternut squash chopped
- 32 oz. vegetable stock
- ¼ tsp. allspice
- ¼ tsp. cayenne
- 1 tsp. onion powder
- 1 tsp. garlic powder
- 1 tsp. salt
- 1 tsp. pepper
- 1 container Kite Hill vegan cream cheese

Directions

- Melt the butter in a large pot, and add the onion, celery, carrot, potatoes, and squash
- Mix thoroughly
- Pour vegetable stock over vegetables and bring to a boil
- Reduce heat to low, cover pot, and simmer 40 minutes
- Transfer the soup to a blender, and blend until smooth. Return to pot, and add salt, pepper, allspice, onion powder, garlic powder, cayenne and salt
- With a hand held mixer mix cream cheese and blend

My Dad's Meat Sauce

- 1 pound ground beef
- 1 onion
- 4 cloves garlic, minced
- 1 small green bell pepper, diced
- 1 28 ounce can diced tomatoes
- 1 16 ounce can tomato paste
- 2 tsp. dried oregano
- 2 tsp. dried basil
- 1 tsp. salt
- 1 ½ tsp. black pepper
- Most importantly- sugar

Directions

- Cook ground beef till just browning
- Mix all ingredients and slow simmer
- Add sugar to your sweetness preference

My father passed away January 2010. In the earlier years of my life there was only one day that my mother worked away from home and that was on Sundays. I know my dad was able to cook many things but every Sunday we all knew it was time for his meat sauce. I always looked forward to spending Sundays with my Dad and today still those wonderful memories all surface with the aroma of his sauce. It is one of my many happy memories of him. My hope is that when people recreate this recipe that they can create memories they too can associate with the same smell and feel that same warmth in my heart that I get whenever I cook it now.   In loving memory, Kellie Koch

Vegan Red "Meat" Sauce

- 1 onion
- 1 small green bell pepper, diced
- 2 28 oz. fire roasted diced tomatoes
- 1 28 oz. chunky tomato sauce
- 12 tsp. dried oregano
- 2 tsp. dried basil
- 1 ½ tsp. black pepper
- 1 jar organic garlic
- 3 tsp. salt
- 1 tsp. red pepper flakes
- 1 tsp. black pepper
- 1 tsp. Italian seasoning
- 1 tsp. herbs de province
- 1 pound vegan Gardein burger crumples

Directions

- Cook garlic and onions in olive oil
- Mix all ingredients and slow simmer. Add garlic and onions and stir
- Add vegan burger crumples

Favorite Holiday Stuffing

- 1 Pkg. Brownberry Bread Cubes
- 1 Pkg. pork sausage (I like Jimmy Deans)
- 1 Carton Vegetable Broth
- 1/4 cup Butter
- 1 Large Onion chopped
- 8 oz. Portabella Mushrooms chopped
- 8 oz. Shredded Carrots
- 1 Shredded apple (I Like Granny Smith)
- 1/2 cup dried Cranberries
- 1/2 cup chopped Pecans
- 1/2 tsp. sage
- 1/2 tsp. poultry seasoning

Directions

- Use a 6 Qt. Pan
- Brown sausage, add butter to melt
- Add seasonings, Onions, Mushrooms, Carrots
- Stir until softened, add apple, cranberries and pecans
- Add bread cubes and stir to blend a bit
- Add broth to moisten well. Put in lightly greased casserole dish and keep refrigerated until ready to bake
- Bake 350 for 1 hour or heated through
- Refrigerate leftovers for up to 3 days

Shared by Kay Melson in loving memory of her husband, Jerry

Vegan Holiday Stuffing

- 1 Loaf Organic bread*
- 1 pkg. of Tofurky Italian vegan sausage
- 32 ounces of vegetable broth
- ¼ cup of vegan butter
- 1 large white onion chopped
- 12 oz. portable mushrooms chopped
- 8 oz shredded carrots
- 1 granny smith apple (shredded)
- ½ cup dried cranberries
- ½ cup chopped pecans
- ½ tsp. basil
- ½ tsp. poultry seasoning

Directions

- *Keep bread in fridge for 1 week. We use Wegman's organic rosemary sourdough
- Brown the sausage using the butter
- Take the bread and cut it into small cubes
- Add seasonings, onions, mushrooms and carrots, apple, cranberries and pecans along with breadcrumbs and stir to blend
- Add broth to moisten
- Bake in a 9x13 pan at 350 for 1 hour

"Food is love made tasty"

Delectable Dishes

Burgers

- 12 slices bacon
- 2 pounds lean ground beef
- ¼ cup finely chopped sweet onion
- ¼ cup finely chopped green sweet pepper
- 1 tsp. ground black pepper
- ½ tsp. seasoned salt
- 12 slices bacon
- 2 pounds lean ground beef
- ½ tsp. ground sage
- 2 eggs, beaten
- 1/4 cup mild or hot barbecue sauce
- 8 hamburger buns, split
- Sliced onions
- Bar-b-q sauce
- ½ tsp. ground sage
- 2 eggs, beaten

Directions

- Cook bacon in a large skillet over medium heat until crisp. Transfer to paper towels to drain Let cool slightly; crumble
- Combine bacon, ground beef, beaten eggs, onion, sweet pepper, black pepper, seasoned salt, and sage in a large bowl; mix well. Shape into 6 patties about 1 inch thick
- Grill for 18 to 20 minutes or when center registers 160 degree F, turning burgers once
- Optional - Brush with the 1/4 cup barbecue sauce the last 5 minutes of grilling
- Serve the burgers on buns with sliced onions and, if desired, additional barbecue sauce
- Makes 6 burgers

Kens Vegan Black Bean Burgers

- 3 cups black beans
- 1 cup rice
- 1 tbsp. olive oil
- 1 onion finely chopped
- 1 large shallot
- 2 cloves garlic
- Paprika
- 1 ½ tsp. onion powder
- ½ tsp. garlic powder
- 1/8 tsp. allspice
- 1 ¼ rolled oats
- 1 tbsp. chipotle peppers in adobe sauce
- 1 ½ tsp. salt
- Ground pepper
- 3 tablespoons liquid smoke
- 1 ½ cup bread crumbs

Directions

- Cook rice for 20 minutes/water 2 cups
- Caramelize onions
- Sauté
- Olive oil, onion, shallot, garlic, paprika, onion powder, garlic powder, allspice…cook till onions are brown
- Add all non sauté ingredients to a food processor plus ½ cup rolled oats, pulse till all ingredients are well mixed (slightly chunky)
- Then add onion sauté and stir
- Chill mixture 30 min
- Oven at 400
- ½ cup burger mixture
- Skillet 10 minutes each side on # 6

Pasta and Peas

- 1 medium onion chopped
- ½ can tomato paste
- 1 can peas
- Salt and black pepper to taste
- Basil
- ½ to 2/3 lb. small seashell macaroni

Directions

- In a 6 or 8 quart pot, sauté the chopped onion with a little olive oil, salt and pepper until golden and translucent
- Add the tomato paste and basil. Let it simmer a bit – continue stirring it
- Add the can of peas. Squash some of the peas with a spoon
- Add 2-3 cans (using the pea can) of water and mix in the tomato paste
- Then fill the pot ½ to ¾ with water
- In a separate pot, cook macaroni until ¾ cooked. Drain the macaroni and put in the pot with peas
- Cook 5-10 minutes until macaroni is cooked, adding water as needed

Contributed in loving memory of my mother-in-law Mary Scarcelli who truly knew how to create wonderful family meals in every way! This will definitely warm you up on a cold winter day and it is even better the next day!   Betsy Scarcelli

"Every bite triggers a wonderful memory"

Spaghetti & Meatballs w/ Sausage

- 1-2 lbs Ground beef
- Diced onions
- 1-2 eggs depending on amount of beef
- Bread crumbs
- Salt/pepper

Combine ingredients above and make into balls. Set aside

In a large stock pot:
- 2-4 Large cans of tomato sauce
- 1 small can of tomato paste
- Italian seasonings

Mild & hot Italian sausage (Hatfield) cut into 2-4 in pieces. And add to sauce

Cover and let simmer on the stove all day (this can also be done in the crock pot)

In loving memory of my brother Greg. Ellen Friend

Vegan Spaghetti and Meatballs

- 1 onion
- 1 small green bell pepper, diced
- 2 28 oz. fire roasted diced tomatoes
- 1 28 oz. chunky tomato sauce
- 12 tsp. dried oregano
- 2 tsp. dried basil
- 1 ½ tsp. black pepper
- 1 jar organic garlic
- 3 tsp. salt
- 1 tsp. red pepper flakes
- 1 tsp. black pepper
- 1 tsp. Italian seasoning
- 1 tsp. herbs de province
- 1 lb. vegan Gardein meatless meatballs
- 1 lb. Tofurky spicy sausage
- 1 lb. organic pasta*

Directions

- Cook garlic and onions in olive oil
- In water, cook pasta to taste (5-7 min)
- Remove cooked noodles and spray down with cool water
- Mix all sauce ingredients and slow simmer. Add garlic and onions and stir
- Add vegan Gardein meatless meatballs and Tofurky spicy sausage

Mom's Chicken & Gravy

- 1 lb. chicken
- ¼ cup butter (melted slow)
- 3-5 bouillon cubes
- Salt & pepper to taste

Directions

- Using thin sliced chicken breasts, dip each into flour (with salt & pepper) and put into pan for a few minutes until lightly browned on each side. Add more butter to the pan if necessary
- When chicken in ½ way cooked remove from pan and set aside
- Sauté onions in the pan, add flour (no more than ½ cup) until all liquid is soaked
- Add 3-5 chicken bouillon cubes (or broth) as the flour starts to turn brownish add water slowly and keep stirring (no bumps). If using broth you may not need water. The water is for the bouillon cube. Increase flour until desired thickness of gravy
- Add the chicken back to the pan. Cover and simmer on low for 30 mins

In loving memory of my brother Greg.   Ellen Friend

Ken's Vegan "Chicken" & Gravy

- 4 tbsp. Vegan butter
- ¼ tsp. Poultry seasoning
- ¼ tsp. Salt
- 1 ½ cups Vegetable broth
- ¼ cup organic all purpose flour

Directions

- Melt butter in a saucepan. Once melted add in flour, poultry seasoning, salt and vegetable broth gradually stirring with a whisk
- Cook for 5 minutes adding flour and or vegetable broth to desired consistency
- Chicken use Gardein breaded turkey cutlets

Denny's Favorite Tuna Fish Casserole

- 1 can Campbell's® Condensed Cream of Mushroom Soup or Campbell's® Condensed 98% Fat Free Cream of Mushroom Soup
- 1/2 cup milk
- 2 cans (about 5 ounces each) tuna in water, drained
- 4 ounces (about 2 cups) medium egg noodles, cooked and drained
- 1 cup crushed potato chips

Directions

- Heat the oven to 400°F. Stir the soup, milk, tuna and noodles in a 1 ½ quart casserole
- Bake the tuna mixture for 20 minutes or until hot and bubbling. Stir the tuna mixture. Sprinkle with the crushed chips
- Bake for 5 minutes or until the chips are golden brown

In memory of my brother Denny
Karolee Schloth

Vegan Tuna Fish Casserole

- 2 cup raw sunflower seeds
- 1 cup celery, minced
- 1 cup pickles, minced
- 1 cup red onion, minced
- 2 tbsp. freshly squeezed lemon juice
- 4 tbsp. pickle juice
- 2 tbsp. vegan mayonnaise
- 4 tbsp. Dulce
- 1/4 cup flour
- 2 cups vegetable broth
- 12 oz. noodles
- 2 cups Daiya shredded cheese
- Bread crumbs

Directions

- Preheat oven to 400 degrees and lightly grease a 9x13 pan
- Cook the noodles according to the package directions. Drain and add pasta to prepared pan
- Heat vegetable broth and bring to a simmer, add cheese and stirring constantly. Tuna
- In a food processor, combine all ingredients and process till a paste texture
- Place all ingredients in a large bowl except broth. Mix thoroughly. Add vegetable broth, mix and place in pan. Sprinkle with bread crumbs and back 30 minutes

Jamie's Favorite Chili

- 2 lb ground beef
- 1 lb pork sausage
- 2 28 Oz cans diced fire roasted tomatoes
- 1/2 sweet pepper
- 2 cans black beans
- 2 cans canneloni beans
- 1 lg onion
- 4 cloves garlic, minced
- Salt/pepper
- 1 1/2 tsp. liquid smoke
- 1 tbsp. Worcestershire sauce
- 1/3 bottle dark beer
- 6 hot cherry peppers (in jar)
- 1/4 c juice of cherry peppers
- 1/2 tsp. chipotle chili pepper powder
- 1/2 tsp. cumin
- 1/2 tsp. cayenne

Directions

- Diced onions & sweet pepper
- Brown ground meat, sausage, adding onions and sweet pepper.
- Drain fat from meat & add back to pot
- Add spices: salt, pepper, cumin, cayenne, chipotle chili powder, stir well
- Add black beans, cannelloni beans, tomatoes & cherry peppers, stir well
- Next add liquid smoke, beer, Worcestershire sauce & Franks hot sauce, stir well
- Last add garlic (we love raw garlic. if you'd like a more mild flavor, sauté the garlic with the onions

In loving memory of my son, Jamie

Jamie loved food & chili was one of his favorites. I could always ensure a visit from school if I text him it was simmering. Joanne Braunsberg

Spicy Vegan Chili

- 2 tbsp. olive oil
- 1 yellow onion (diced)
- 1 red pepper (diced)
- 1 yellow pepper (diced)
- 2 jalapeno pepper (diced)
- 5 cloves of garlic
- 1 28 oz. can fire Roasted tomatoes
- 2 cups vegetable stock
- ½ tsp. cayenne
- 1 15 oz. can black beans
- 1 15 oz. can kidney beans
- 1 bag frozen corn
- 1 15 oz. can canelli beans

Directions

- Cook onion in oil till translucent on a medium flame
- Add garlic and cook another 5 minutes
- Add all ingredients but beans and corn and simmer for 30 minutes
- Add beans and corn and salt and pepper to taste
- Simmer for 30 minutes

Mom Mom's Eggplant Caponata

- 1 eggplant, peeled & cut into 1/2-inch cubes
- salt to taste
- 1/4 cup olive oil, divided
- 1 cup finely chopped celery
- 1 onion, finely chopped
- 1 clove garlic, minced
- 1 1/2 tablespoons drained capers
- 12 green olives, pitted and coarsely chopped
- 1 1/2 cups canned plum tomatoes, drained and coarsely chopped
- 2 tsp. minced fresh parsley, or to taste
- 1 tbsp. tomato paste
- 1 tsp. minced oregano
- 2 tsp. red wine vinegar
- 2 tsp. white sugar
- 1 tsp. salt
- Ground black pepper to taste
- 1 1/2 tbsp. drained capers

Directions

- Toss eggplant with salt and place in a colander set over a bowl. Let sit, about 30 minutes. Rinse and pat dry
- Heat 2 tablespoons olive oil in a large skillet over medium heat. Add celery; cook, stirring often, until softened, about 4 minutes. Add onion and garlic; cook and stir until onion is soft and lightly golden, about 5 minutes. Transfer mixture to a bowl using a slotted spoon
- Heat remaining 2 tablespoons olive oil in the skillet. Add eggplant and cook, stirring constantly, until lightly browned, 5 to 7 minutes. Stir in celery mixture, tomatoes, olives, capers, tomato paste, and oregano. Bring to a boil; reduce heat to low and simmer uncovered until caponata is thickened, about 15 minutes

- Season caponata with vinegar, sugar, salt, and black pepper. Transfer to a serving bowl and garnish with parsley

My Mom Mom or as the world new her Gilda (Judy) Intrieri was the matriarch of our family born of Italian descent the product of a traditional arranged marriage and had a gracious heart. Mom Mom always made you feel special and welcomed anytime you stopped by whether it was a planned visit or random. She always had fresh baked bread, pastries and of course classic Italian dishes that my grandfather and her grew up eating. Food was always important and mealtime was special, looked forward to, not a stop and go thing that it is today. It was a time to slow down, pause and really talk and share what was going on in your life and here what was going on in other family members lives. It was how we stay connected and supported each other, it was a source of healing, courage and confidence to go out and challenge the world because it gave you a sense of where you came from, who you are and that you were loved unconditionally. This recipe for Caponata is one of my all time favorites that Mom Mom would have on hand most of the time, it is very versatile it can be eaten at room temperature with crusty bread, used as a sauce for pasta, a side dish with meat or as a relish for chicken or fish. Every time I eat this it takes me back to my Mom Mom's house and I feel that sense of love and family, I hope you enjoy this recipe and it makes you feel the same way.   Chef Ben Vozzo

Pad Thai

Pad Thai
- 8 ounces flat rice noodles
- 3 tbsp. oil
- 3 cloves garlic, minced
- 8 ounces uncooked shrimp or chicken
- 2 eggs
- 1 cup fresh bean sprouts
- 1 red bell pepper, thinly sliced
- 1/2 cup dry roasted peanuts

Sauce
- 3 tbsp. fish sauce
- 1 tbsp. low-sodium soy sauce
- 5 tbsp. light brown sugar
- 2 tbsp. rice vinegar
- 1 tbsp. hot sauce to taste
- 2 tbsp. creamy peanut butter

Topping Options
- 3 green onions, chopped
- 2 limes

Directions

- Cook noodles according to package instructions, just until tender. Rinse to cool
- Mix the sauce ingredients together. Set aside
- Heat 1½ tablespoons of oil in a large saucepan or wok over medium-high heat
- Add the shrimp or chicken, garlic and bell pepper. The shrimp will cook quickly, about 1-2 minutes on each side, or until pink
- Push everything to the side of the pan. Add a little more oil and add the beaten eggs Scramble the eggs, breaking them into small pieces with a spatula as they cook
- Add noodles, sauce, bean sprouts and peanuts to the pan (save some peanuts for topping) Toss everything to combine
- Top with green onions, extra peanuts and lime wedges. Serve immediately

Vegan Pad Thai

- 8 oz. dried rice noodles
- 2 tbsp. of vegetable oil
- 200g of firm tofu in thin slices
- 2 carrots cut into small cubes
- 2 tbsp. soy sauce
- 2 tbsp. sugar
- ½ cup of water
- 3 tbsp. chopped peanuts
- 1 cup snow peas
- 1 tbsp. a sesame seeds
- Juice of half a lime

Directions

- Put the noodles in a bowl of water and cover with hot water
- Let them sit for 15 minutes to soften. Drain well
- Pour the oil into a pan (or wok) and brown the tofu for 5 minutes
- In a bowl, combine the soy sauce, water and sugar
- Add the carrot and the soy sauce mixture. Pour in the lime juice
- Cook another 5 minutes over high heat
- Add the noodles, peanuts and the sweet peas. Cook another 4 minutes
- Serve in a bowl & sprinkle with sesame seeds

Eve's Golden Chicken Cheddar Bake

- 2 lbs. cooked chicken shredded into pieces
- 1½ cups celery chopped
- 8 oz. shredded cheddar cheese
- ¾ cup thousand Island dressing
- ¼ cup almonds
- 1 tsp. salt
- 2 tbsp. butter melted
- ½ cup corn flakes

Directions

- Combine ingredients together
- Place in baking dish
- Mix flakes with melted butter
- Sprinkle on top
- Bake 350 for about 35 minutes

Dedicated in loving memory to my mom, who I miss and love so very much.
Rachael Morrison

Vegan Chicken Cheddar Bake

- 1 -2 pkg. Gardein chicken, straight from the package
- 1½ cups celery chopped
- 8 oz. Daiya shredded cheddar cheese
- ¾ cup Daiya thousand Island dressing
- 2 tbsp. vegan butter melted
- ½ cup organic corn flakes
- ¼ cup almonds
- 1 tsp. salt

Directions

- Preheat oven to 350
- Combine ingredients together
- Place in baking dish
- Mix corn flakes with melted butter
- Sprinkle mixer on top
- Bake 35 minutes

Lasagna

- 3 cups ricotta cheese
- ¾ cup grated Parmesan cheese
- 2 egg
- 1 ib. ground beef
- 2 jars Prego® Three Cheese Italian Sauce
- 12 cooked lasagna noodles, drained
- 12 ounces shredded mozzarella cheese (about 3 cups)

Directions

- Preheat oven to 400°
- Stir the ricotta cheese, ½ cup Parmesan cheese and eggs in a medium bowl and set it aside. Season the beef as desired
- In a saucepan over medium-high heat, cook the beef until it's browned, stirring often to break up the meat. Pour off any fat. Stir the sauce in the saucepan
- Spoon 2 cups beef mixture into a 13x9 baking dish. Top with 4 lasagna noodles, half the ricotta cheese mixture and half the mozzarella. Repeat the layers. Top with the remaining 4 lasagna noodles, remaining beef mixture and the remaining Parmesan cheese
- Cook for 30 minutes or until the lasagna is hot
- Let stand for 10 minutes before cutting

Ken's Vegan Lasagna

- 1 box of lasagna noodles (cook as per directions)
- Sauce (see vegan red sauce recipe)
- 2 packages mushrooms, sliced
- 2 tbsp. minced garlic
- 3 containers kite hill ricotta cheese
- 1 box fresh spinach (if desired)

Directions

- Preheat oven to 400
- Cook noodles as per directed
- Place 2 tablespoons minced garlic with ½ cup water in a large skillet for 3 minutes on medium/high heat. Add mushrooms and cook till tender…drain
- Line bottom of lasagna dish with sauce then a layer of noodles, mushrooms, spinach and ricotta, add more sauce and continue for 3-4 layers.
- Top with remaining sauce
- Bake 40 minutes

"Learn how to cook- try new recipes, learn from your mistakes, be fearless, and above all have fun!"

— Julia Child

Tricks & "Truisms"

Substitutions

Below are options for what to substitute as you are converting a recipe of our own from the traditional way to a more healthy way.

Traditional Ingredients	Alternative Options
1 tsp. cornstarch	2 tsp. of flour as a substitute
1 egg	3 oz applesauce
1 egg	1 tsp. of ground flax seed plus 1-2 t of water
Egg for breakfast	Tofu (many ways to prepare and serve)
Eggs as binding agent	Oat or soy flour, rolled oats, cooked oatmeal, bread crumbs, instant potato flakes, nut butters, tomato paste
1 cup milk	1 cup of unsweetened coconut, almond or soy
Heavy cream	Organic evaporated coconut milk
1 cup of sugar	1 cup of honey
1 cup of sugar	½ cup agave
Parmesan Cheese or Salt as g seasoning	Nutritional yeast as a garnish or seasoning
Honey	Maple syrup or agave nectar
Sugar	Organic sugar, beet sugar, unbleached cane
Butter or margarine	Vegan brands in organic isle
Milk chocolate	Dark Chocolate
Cocoa Powder	Non-Dairy Cocoa Powder
Ice Cream	Soy, almond or cashew based ice cream
Bread	Organic bread (has fewer ingredients)
Meat	Organic options and also vegan brands for all in organic isles

Measurement "Truisms"

1 tablespoon (tbsp..) = 3 teaspoons (tsp.)
2 tbsp. = 1 ounce
1/8 cup = 2 tbsp.
1/4 cup = 4 tbsp.
1/3 cup = 5 tbsp. + 1 tsp.
1/2 cup = 8 tbsp.
3/4 cup = 12 tbsp.
1 cup = 48 tsp.
1 cup = 16 tbsp.
8 fluid ounces (fl oz) = 1 cup
1 pint (pt) = 2 cups
1 quart (qt) = 2 pints or 4 cups
4 cups = 1 quart
1 gallon (gal) = 4 quarts
1 ounce (dry) = 2 tbsp.
16 ounces (oz) = 1 pound (lb)

Splittin' the V's vs. the Peas — Our Interpretation

Splitting' the V's vs. the Peas…get it?   Split peas…I know, bad right! Well anyway, the true understanding and differences between the V's, vegetarians and vegans, is and has become incredibly blurred. The way we have come to understand them is as follows:

Vegetarian - A true vegetarian does not consume any animal products into their body. This includes milk, dairy, eggs, meat etc. There are many versions of vegetarians but in the true sense of the word they don't ingest any animal products. A vegetarian, will however, still wear items of leather or use other products made from animal products.

Vegan - A vegan does not consume any animal products, nor do they use or wear any animal products. They consume plant based, whole food products like beans, potatoes, greens, vegetables, fruits and grains.

Thank you

Recipes are often coveted and considered treasures that are passed down from one generation to the next. Sharing something so engrained in a family's culture is a true act of unconditional love. I believe lending a legacy to begin a new tradition in another family and generation is a priceless act and something I take incredibly serious. By doing so, it's a true test of respect and perhaps it can be taken as a ceremonial "inviting someone into your extended family" without smoking the peace pipe to seal the union, like in Native American culture.

So the thank you that I extend to everyone that so generously invited us into his or her extended family is with the sincerest of gratitude. As you have read, each person holds deep regard and sentimental value to the recipe provided here for your culinary enjoyment. They will forever provide beautiful and somewhat bittersweet memories and are eternally blessed for the love they share with the loved one that presents them with each tasty bite.

Joanne Braunsberg	R. Jade McAuliffe	Betsy Scarcelli
Ellen Friend	Kay Melson	Karolee Schloth
Pam Horowitz	Rachael Morrison	Ben Vozzo
Kellie Koch	Aubrey Nicole Riegel	Christine Bentivoglio Worstall

Always give thanks for the food that keeps the good memories flowing…

Family is not just about being from the same tree, it is about the roots from many trees that connect, entwine & nurture.

Ken Bell & Marcy Stone

About the Authors

Ken Bell

Ken's background is science based as an Exercise Physiologist by formal training. He has been the Anatomist for Yoga teacher training programs, and is certified in Plant Based Nutrition from Cornell University. In addition, he is also a certified Usui Reiki Master/Teacher, tai chi, and meditation and yoga instructor. He has taught yoga and meditation internationally.

Ken has a unique and skillful way of offering wellness and conscious living alternatives, and strives to inspire others in their journey of self-discovery. He is an author of a fitness booklet and a featured contributor to health and wellness websites including MindBodyGreen. To learn more about Ken go to www.kenbell.yoga.

Marcy Stone

Marcy is an accomplished writer and author of "The Voice of an Angel", sharing her journey following the tragic death of her youngest daughter, and is a motivational speaker as well as an Intuitive Life Guide for over 15 years. She is the creator of The Soulfull Paths® technique, holds advanced certificates in several healing modalities and is a yoga instructor in addition to having over 17 years of business leadership experience.

She is a lifetime student of the healing arts and brings her passion for growth and self-empowerment into her work and life. Marcy's life and career experiences have helped her realize and teach the true importance of balance in life — physically, mentally, emotionally, spiritually and energetically. To learn more about Marcy go to www.marcystone.com

"A recipe has no soul. You, as the cook, must bring the soul to the recipe."
-Thomas Keller

Made in the USA
Middletown, DE
14 February 2019